SECURING SALESFORCE DIGITAL EXPERIENCES

SECURING SALESFORCE DIGITAL EXPERIENCES

BASED ON A TRUE STORY ABOUT HOW MY CUSTOMER'S SALESFORCE DIGITAL EXPERIENCE SITE GOT HACKED AND WHAT I LEARNED FROM IT.

MATT MEYERS

SALESFORCE CERTIFIED TECHNICAL ARCHITECT

Important Disclaimer
This publication contains materials based on actual true events that took place, but names and certain details about those circumstances have been changed to protect the identity of those involved and for other educational purposes. All names of companies and people depicted in this publication are purely fictional, and any similarities to actual people, companies, or situations are purely coincidental in nature.

This publication contains materials designed to assist readers in securing their Salesforce Digital Experience sites for educational purposes only. While the publisher and author have made every attempt to verify that the information provided in this book is correct and up to date, the publisher and author assume no responsibility for any error, inaccuracy, or omission.

The advice, examples, strategies, and best practices contained herein are not suitable for every situation. The materials contained herein are not intended to represent or guarantee you will achieve your desired results, and the publisher and author make no such guarantee. Neither the publisher nor author shall be liable for damages arising therefrom. No system can be made 100 percent secure, and there are many different factors that must be considered when securing any system, including Salesforce beyond the control of the publisher and author.

The company confirms sole responsibility for the contents of this book.

This book is dedicated to all the Salesforce administrators, consultants, developers, and architects out there who work many long, hard hours, burning the candle at both ends.

I would like to thank Tom Leddy, Martin Humpolec, and the Salesforce Well-Architected team and community for their inspiration and guidance.

CONTENTS

Foreword · xi
Preface · xiv
Prologue · xvii

Chapter 1   Setting the Scene · · · · · · · · · · · · · · · · · · · 1
Chapter 2   Salesforce Digital Experiences · · · · · · · · · · 7
Chapter 3   Salesforce Sharing · · · · · · · · · · · · · · · · · 11
                    Guest User Sharing · · · · · · · · · · · · · · · 14
                    Salesforce to the Rescue! · · · · · · · · · · · 26
                    A New Guest Sharing Model · · · · · · · · 27
                    The Problem with @AuraEnabled · · · · · 32
Chapter 4   Ensuring Customer Data Security · · · · · · · · 37
                    Give Read-Only Access via Guest Sharing
                    Rules · 47
                    The Problem with Adding Apex Classes
                    to the Guest User Profile · · · · · · · · · · · · 48
                    Add Without Sharing to Apex Classes · 49
Chapter 5   Solving the Problem · · · · · · · · · · · · · · · · · 51
                    Step 1: Identify the Hole · · · · · · · · · · · · 53

Step 2: Plug the Hole · · · · · · · · · · · · · · 55
Step 3: Clean Up the Data · · · · · · · · · · 57
Step 4: Validate and Reactivate · · · · · · · 58
This Was Only the Beginning · · · · · · · · 59
Chapter 6   The Real Cost of a Data Breach · · · · · · · · · · 61
What Can Be Done to Avoid
a Breach? · 62
Chapter 7   Conclusion · 70

Appendix A: Salesforce Well-Architected · · · · · · · · · · 73

Appendix B: How Does Well-Architected Help to
Prevent Data Breaches? · 78
Before Anything, a Salesforce Solution
Should Be Secure · · · · · · · · · · · · · · · · · · · 78
Organizational Security · · · · · · · · · · · · · 80
Session Security · 82
Data Security · 83
Salesforce Solutions Should Be
Compliant · 85
Ethical Standards · · · · · · · · · · · · · · · · · · · 86
Like Driving on the Bridge, Salesforce
Solutions Should Be Reliable · · · · · · · · 87
Using the Well-Architected Framework
in the Real World · · · · · · · · · · · · · · · · · · · 88
A Well-Architected Secure Solution · · · 90

BONUS #1: Recommended Best Practices for Securing
Your Salesforce Data in Digital Experiences and Sites · 92
Salesforce Sharing Settings · · · · · · · · · 92

Salesforce File Settings · · · · · · · · · · · · · ·97
Salesforce Digital Experiences
Settings ·98

BONUS #2: How to Ethically Hack Your Salesforce Digital
Site to Protect Your Data · 110

BONUS #3: What's the Big Deal About Viruses in
Salesforce and Why Should You Care? · · · · · · · · · · · · · 112

References· 114
Resources · 116
About the Author· 118

FOREWORD

The first time I met Matt Meyers was during a virtual presentation about the Salesforce Well-Architected framework that I gave to the San Francisco Architects Trailblazer Community Group, which he had cofounded a few months earlier. As I was explaining the framework to the group, Matt immediately recognized the value of the Secure topic and hung out afterward to chat with me some more.

He told me about his company's focus on helping organizations assess their current security configuration to identify and close gaps that can be exploited by hackers and cybercriminals. We hit it off instantly, and I was fortunate to have an opportunity to meet him in person at a conference in Paris a couple months later. Since then, I've seen Matt give numerous presentations about security-related topics, and we've continued to have great discussions about security best practices as well. As a result, I've developed a deep respect for Matt as both a subject matter expert and a friend.

Securing enterprise systems is one of the most complicated tasks in all of IT. Security experts are in a constant battle against criminals who would love nothing more than to find a way to profit from stealing data about an organization or its customers. These criminals are often part of intricate networks that utilize advanced communication techniques to share the latest tools and methods with each other. Any hacker who discovers a new vulnerability can make it available to the masses within seconds if they so choose. (Fortunately, there are plenty of ethical hackers out there as well, but you can never be too vigilant.)

On the other side of the equation, security experts also need to make sure that they aren't preventing legitimate users from accessing the data they need to do their jobs. If business users can't access all the information they need, they might end up making bad or uninformed decisions, which can negatively impact their organization's operations. And if customers aren't able to access the data they need to be able to work with an organization, they'll likely bring their business to a competitor.

So a security expert needs to stay up to date on the latest tools and methods employed by hackers and cybercriminals and respond accordingly while also understanding an organization's user personas and business processes so they can configure the systems they're responsible for in a way that ensures that everyone who logs in really is who they say they are, can access only the data they need to access, and is restricted from accessing information they shouldn't have access to.

In this book, Matt provides practical advice to people who have to deal with this complex balancing act on a daily basis. He uses real-world scenarios and step-by-step guidance, covering topics like how to prevent security breaches and also what to do if one occurs. It also has something for everyone. If you're a security professional, you'll find this book to be a valuable resource that you can refer to as you're building or assessing your organization's security model. If you're not a security professional, the stories and guidance will help you understand more about the complexities related to the work that your organization's security team does. In either case, I hope you'll enjoy reading it as much as I did.

Tom Leddy

PREFACE

Securing Salesforce Digital Experiences is based on a real experience that I faced where an ethical hacker hacked one of my customer's data in Salesforce due to a misconfiguration of their security settings. This had a huge impact on my customer as well as the people that trusted them with their personal data. I felt it was important that others heard the story so that they could learn from it and prevent this from happening to them as well.

I am a Salesforce Certified Technical Architect (CTA) and have spent the past eighteen years of my career learning everything I could about Salesforce. For the past five years, I've done nothing but focus on Salesforce security. Currently, I am focusing on educating people about Salesforce security and how they can better protect their data and customers in Salesforce.

This book is composed of two main parts. The first covers my personal experience waking up and realizing we had been hacked, what events transpired, and how we resolved the issue. I will walk you through the history of the Salesforce Digital Experience guest user security issues and how Salesforce worked to remedy those problems. Then in the second part of the book I discuss what you can do to improve your Salesforce security to protect your data.

This is my first book, and I don't plan for it to be my last. In preparation for writing the book, I spent countless hours researching and duplicating exactly how the ethical hacker was able to penetrate my customer's Digital Experience site. I went so far as to set up my own Digital Experience site that looked and felt real so that I could make it as accurate as possible during my research.

I not only wanted to understand how the attacker performed the attack, but I also wanted to appreciate the history of the Salesforce guest user and what events transpired when Salesforce released numerous features to lock down the security of the guest user. I have always felt it is important to understand the history of events so that we know where we have been and do not make the same mistakes again. I combed through pages upon pages of Salesforce's release notes and documentation to make sure that I got every detail right.

During my research, I also wondered, how big of a problem is this? Did people already know about this, or was this just an isolated incident? To gain these answers, I decided to travel around the United States and internationally, presenting at local Salesforce Dreamin' events, informing people about my story, and showing them how a hacker performed this attack. During each session, I polled the audience to better understand their awareness of Salesforce security in general. To my surprise, I found most people were overconfident about the security of their Salesforce implementations, and only a select few even knew about this type of attack. This helped me gain more insight into the problem. My hope is that many people and organizations will benefit from this book.

Finally, it wasn't enough that I told the story of what happened. I wanted to provide a pathway so others knew what they could do to prevent this and similar attacks in the future. To do this, I sought out architect ambassadors and evangelists for Well-Architected to better understand Salesforce's Well-Architected framework and how it could be used to help others secure their Salesforce environments and data.

I truly hope this book is helpful to you so you can be more aware of what you should do to secure your data in Salesforce and what tools can help you implement a fortified security program.

PROLOGUE

It was just like any other day. I got out of bed and stumbled into the kitchen and started boiling water in the kettle. (I am just like the millions of other people in the world who must have their coffee as soon as they get out of bed, except I am a bit particular. I mostly drink coffee for the taste, so I use a French press because I've found that it gives you the best control over your coffee. I've discovered that a medium-roast Colombian coffee paired with the French press makes for the perfect cup. I'm not talking about what you find in the grocery store, but the real thing straight from Colombia.)

While I was waiting for that black magic to brew, I put a pot of hot water on the stove to cook up some oatmeal or something else that cooks quickly and doesn't require too much of my time so I can carry on with the rest of my morning.

I powered up my MacBook Pro and checked my email and calendar to see what my day looked like. I was expecting the usual mundane and time-consuming process of deleting all the newsletters and other junk that piles up in my inbox overnight to find the one or two emails where someone has a legitimate question that I need to answer. But this day was different.

What was this?

> Re: URGENT—Potential PII data leak found by ethical hacker

My heart immediately sank!

This was one of those things you just read about, but it doesn't actually happen to you until it does. At this point, I completely forgot about my coffee and oatmeal cooking on the stove; my focus was entirely on what was glaring in front of me.

I thought to myself, what happened? How bad is it? Is this real?

The email read:

> *Hello Team,*
>
> *I was just contacted by an ethical hacker who informed me that he was able to suc-*

cessfully retrieve a large number of customer records that included private and personal information from our Salesforce public-facing customer support portal.

We have yet to confirm his claims, but we are taking them very seriously.

Apparently, he used several manual detection techniques that uncovered some public-facing APIs that allowed him to retrieve some of our customer records without having to authenticate.

I don't have to tell you how serious this is. We have already reported this to the executive leadership team and will be having a meeting today to discuss the potential impacts and how we can validate these claims.

Please be ready to jump on a call within the next hour or so.

Regards,
Sara Wilson
Director of Health Services
First Health Group Inc.

Obviously, I've changed the name and some of the details for privacy reasons, but the email and the situation were real.

How could this have happened? We were so careful. We always reviewed all our code and settings and made certain there were no security issues before releasing changes to our production systems.

CHAPTER 1

SETTING THE SCENE

To give a little background, I've been working as a Salesforce consultant for almost two decades helping customers transform their business and customer experience.

I had been on this project only for a few months, but my customer had been using Salesforce for about six years. About five years ago, they decided to move to Salesforce Digital Experiences from a legacy system to provide a better and more streamlined support experience for their customers.

The project took about a year to complete, but as soon as it launched they saw an immediate customer satisfaction improvement. Customers could access the portal and search for relevant help articles to answer their questions without even having to contact support.

As a healthcare provider, they had many products that required customers to submit information, such as applying for a health care plan, submitting claims, or matching them with the right provider. Customers were asked to provide their personal information such as name, phone number, email, birthday, social security number, income, and so forth.

In the previous system, my customer had to first create an account to log on before they were asked to complete this information, causing many to turn away before starting the process. Now they could start an application without having to log on.

It was only once the online form was completed that the customer's patients were asked to create an account. If a patient didn't have time to complete the form or abandoned the process, the provider would email the customer a link to finish later since the first thing they had to enter was their email address.

Prior to implementing this process, more than half the applications that people submitted were never completed, but with this new process, we saw an increase of application completions to over 75 percent.

Everything was going great. The business was happy, and there were no issues until that day.

As it turned out, the very solution that was so benefi-cial in providing increased customer satisfaction was also the reason why we were now leaking customers' private and confidential information to the public inter-net. Little did they know, their Salesforce environment had been misconfigured causing data to be leaked to the public internet.

Suddenly, I smelled something burning. It was my oat-meal! Through all the excitement, I had completely forgotten about it. All the water was gone, and it was mostly black. I didn't even know that was possible. I decided to deal with that later as there were more important things to worry about.

During the meeting, our customer explained to us that the ethical hacker had found that the Salesforce Lightning Experience, which is the user interface that powered our Salesforce Digital Experience portal, used a significant number of microservice application programming interfaces, or APIs, to display the data and user interface layouts. Salesforce did not provide public documentation for these APIs as they were not designed for use directly by Salesforce's customers.

From Salesforce's perspective, these APIs did not pose any more of a security risk than the web pages that the APIs powered since any data that could be accessed from the APIs could also be accessed from the web pages. Salesforce operates under a shared responsible model. Salesforce provides the technology and tools, but it was up to the customer to make sure they had configured Salesforce correctly to not expose any unwanted data via the portal or these APIs.

This is very common in most web applications these days and is not unique to Salesforce. In the past, most web applications would process everything on the server side, meaning the web server had to perform a large amount of processing before the web page could be rendered. With modern web technology, most websites use client-facing APIs executed by the end user's web browser, instead of the web server, enabling the web pages to load much quicker.

Although this is very efficient, the problem we encountered was that our portal was designed based on the premise that there were no APIs available from which the data could be accessed. Salesforce offers their customers many documented and supported APIs that can be used to access customer data, but typically you must authenticate first to use these APIs.

Additionally, there is an option on the user profile called **API Enabled** that, when disabled, blocks all external access to these APIs. This is what we did in our case. We had this option turned off, so as far as we knew, no one could access the data via any APIs.

We had also developed our customer portal Digital Experience in a way that the user interface only displayed specific pages that used custom interface Lightning components, displaying only the exact data that we wanted our users to see instead of using the provided out-of-the-box components that came by default with Salesforce Lightning Experience portals.

Because of this, we had felt confident that no data was being exposed since we were in full control of what was displayed to our users, or so we thought.

 What we didn't know was that even though we had not exposed any pages using the Salesforce default out-of-the-box components, the standard Salesforce pages that let users view data could still be accessed if you knew the right URLs.

Second, we were completely unaware that there were "unpublished" Salesforce APIs that could still access the data even though we had disabled the API Enabled flag on the user profile.

This could prove to be disastrous for any organization.

This scenario is like leaving the back door to your house open, thinking no one will try to enter from your backyard. In reality, they will, and when they do, they have access to everything.

Now imagine this is your business.

You have customer healthcare application information containing personal data that has been made visible to the Salesforce **Guest User**. You had to do this to allow users to submit the applications without authenticating first. You didn't feel this was a security risk because there were no pages where any user could access the data, and you disabled API access.

You thought you had covered all your bases. You were wrong!

Since the Salesforce "unpublished" Lightning API access could not be disabled, you exposed to the world all the personal data for submitted loan applications.

CHAPTER 2

SALESFORCE DIGITAL EXPERIENCES

Before I continue any further, I think it is important that you understand what Salesforce Digital Experiences are and how they work.

If you are already familiar with Digital Experiences then feel free to skip ahead.

Digital Experiences, or what used to be called Salesforce Communities, are public-facing sites or portals that Salesforce clients can use to engage with their customers.

These sites, in many cases, can be configured using Salesforce's drag-and-drop builder to create professional-looking websites without writing a single line of code. Like many other no-code or low-code website builders, there are a large variety of prebuilt out-of-the-box components that you can use to create these sites.

Salesforce Digital Experiences differ from other common website builders in that you also can build custom components that fit your specific branding or other needs. Once built, you can use these custom components interchangeably with the default out-of-the-box components by employing the drag-and-drop builder.

If you so choose, you can even make these custom components blend seamlessly with the Salesforce user interface experience called the Lightning Experience by using their Lightning Design System, which is a collection of user interface design elements such as buttons, images, forms, and other components.

If you would like to learn more about the Lightning Design System, you can find it by going to https://www.lightningdesignsystem.com.

Salesforce Digital Experiences can operate as an unauthenticated public-facing website or have restricted members-only pages that require users to log on before they can access these areas.

Similar to any other site, for a user to log on, they must be assigned a unique account with a username and password. Once they enter the correct credentials, they are admitted to the restricted section, and if the site is configured correctly, they should only see the data that they have been permitted to access by the system administrator.

Since Salesforce has always taken a zero-trust security-first approach, where **Trust** is also one of their core values, visitors accessing the public or unauthenticated pages on the site also require a user to access the pages and data displayed on those pages.

Instead of requiring visitors to log on as this user, any visitor accessing the public site pages is browsing the site as a *guest user*. This guest user has its own set of permissions assigned by the system administrator, designating what pages and data those unauthenticated public visitors can access.

Salesforce provides the ability to create multiple Digital Experience sites, so each site created is also created with its own dedicated guest user.

The guest user was where the root of our problems lay as to why customers' personal and private data was exposed to the public internet.

Since the guest user, for all intents and purposes, is just like any other user in Salesforce, you need to make sure that you have configured all the security settings correctly, or you could be exposing data to anyone accessing the site as the user.

The bigger issue is that unlike a normal user where a single person logs on, hundreds, if not thousands, or even hundreds of thousands of people, could be accessing the site as the guest user, adding to the exposure.

To make matters worse, Salesforce security and data-sharing settings are very granular, which also makes it difficult to understand what data is being shared with any user, including a Digital Experience guest user.

Salesforce realized this was an issue, especially since the guest user had such a large potential exposure, so starting with the Summer '20 release, they began to change how the security and sharing worked with guest users.

Prior to the Salesforce Summer '20 release, the Salesforce guest user had the same sharing model as the other external Digital Experience user types, such as Customer Plus and Partner users.

In the next couple chapters, we will be walking through how the Salesforce sharing model works, and specifically how it used to work for the guest user before Salesforce released changes to help improve the security of how records are shared with the guest user in Digital Experience sites.

CHAPTER 3

SALESFORCE SHARING

Let's take a step back to review how sharing of records and data works in Salesforce.

An object in Salesforce is similar to a table in a database that stores records containing various types of information, such as sales data, customer data, and user data. The Salesforce object model allows you to set the default level of user access to records within Salesforce objects.

Some of this data is not sensitive. You may want every user to be able to see the data, but most of the time, you wouldn't want every user to be able to read or edit by default.

Because of this, Salesforce has a feature called **Sharing Settings** that allows you to set the default level of access that both internal and external (Digital Experience) users have when accessing these objects in Salesforce.

I should also mention that the Sharing Settings only apply to Salesforce Internal, Customer Plus, Partner, and Guest User Salesforce license types. The standard customer license type uses a different type of sharing model called **Sharing Sets**, which I will not be covering in this book. There are also some nuances to how sharing works with the Guest User that I'll be covering later.

The most restrictive sharing permission is **Private**, which means a user would not have access to view any record in an object unless the user "owns" the record, or another user manually shares access.

If you wished for users to be able to view but not edit records in an object, you would use the **Public Read** permission. Or, if you wanted users to be able to view and edit all records in an object, you would use the least restrictive setting **Public Read/Write**.

Because users in Salesforce Digital Experiences are separate from the internal users in a Salesforce environment, Salesforce enabled the sharing features so that you could control the sharing settings individually for both internal Salesforce users and external users in Digital Experiences.

Since Digital Experience users are external to your company, generally you would not want them to have the same default level of access to the data and objects within your Salesforce environment as your internal users.

With these sharing models separated, you can separately set the default visibility for your internal Salesforce users and external Digital Experience users. For example, you may want to make all customer account information **Private** for all your external users by default. In contrast, you may want to allow all your internal users to view customer information by default, setting your internal sharing model for customer information to **Public Read/Only**.

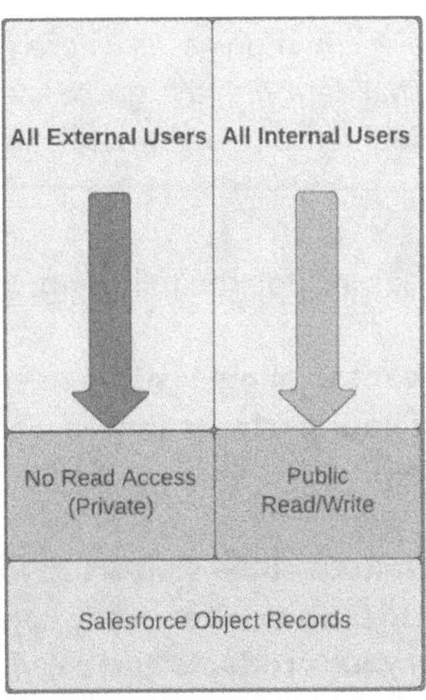

FIGURE 1. AN ILLUSTRATION OF THE SALESFORCE INTERNAL AND EXTERNAL SHARING MODEL.

GUEST USER SHARING

In this section we will be looking back at how you could share records with the Salesforce guest user prior to Salesforce releasing changes in September of 2019 that helped to improve the security of guest user sharing.

The model of separating permissions works well to divide your external and internal user permissions, but one piece of this sharing puzzle that was overlooked until recently: the guest user.

There are many common cases where you may want to share internal data with the guest user so that visitors of your public-facing unauthenticated pages can view specific information.

Some examples include the following:

1. **You want to allow visitors to search the list of your partners they can reach out to for help.**

2. **You want to allow visitors to find specific store locations where they can go to purchase your products and services.**

3. **You have a public-facing e-commerce site and want to allow visitors to search**

through listings of your products, such as on Amazon.com.

4. **You want to publish press releases on your website that are stored in an internal document object your internal users review and publish.**

5. **You have a public-facing knowledge base or help articles that you want public visitors of your site to access.**

These are common examples that many companies use today on their public sites.

This approach works well when you want to share the same data or information with your public site visitors and your authenticated Digital Experience customer, and partner users.

But what if you need to share different data with the public site visitors and your authenticated Digital Experience customer and partner users for the same object in Salesforce? This is where it gets complex because Salesforce allows for very granular controls to control what users can see in Salesforce. As you will see next, great care must be taken when configuring these settings as you could accidentally expose data that was not intended.

For example, you may only want to share select **Global Partners** with public site visitors, but only authenticated users should be able to see all partners.

If you recall earlier, we are only considering Salesforce Internal, Customer Plus, and Partner user License types within this book, as the standard Customer license type uses a different type of sharing called **Sharing Sets**.

For the sake of this example, let's say you have a **Partners** object in Salesforce. In the first example above, you could just set the object's external visibility to **Public Read Only,** since all partner records should be made available to public visitors.

But in this example, you can't set the "partners" object in the external sharing model to **Public Read Only** since the guest user and authenticated Digital Experience users share this model. Setting it to **Public Read Only** would grant read access to all the partner records for both the "guest" unauthenticated site visitors and the authenticated users.

To not expose all partner data to the visitors, the object must be set to **Private**. Then you must set separate criteria-based sharing rules to share only **Global Partner** records with the guest user and then another rule to share all the partners with the authenticated external users.

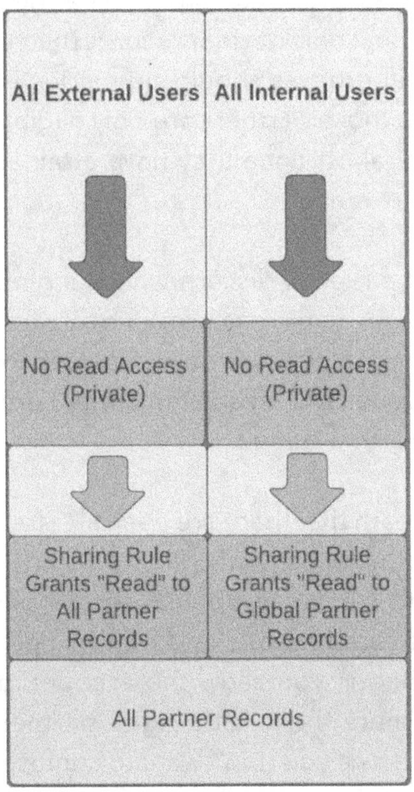

FIGURE 2. ILLUSTRATING HOW ALL PARTNER RECORDS COULD BE SHARED IN SALESFORCE WITH BOTH INTERNAL AND EXTERNAL USERS USING A SHARING RULE.

Okay, that doesn't seem too bad. Only two sharing rules and you are done! Now only Global Partners are visible to the guest user, and only authenticated users can see every partner.

But not so fast! Your customer just added a new requirement that only partner records that have passed an approval process should be made visible to the public, and those partners are only eligible to be put on the global list once they have attained a certain amount of revenue.

To make it easier to discern who is a global partner and who is not, you create a queue to track the global partners. Each global partner is assigned to the Global Partner queue, and those who are not are put in the Regional Partner queue.

Also, you learn that there are special "Strategic" partners that don't necessarily have to make the revenue numbers to be displayed with the global partners. Since these are one-offs and determined by the account manager, you allow the account manager to manually share these "Strategic" partners with the guest user since you don't want to confuse them with being a global partner.

Hopefully you are now starting to understand how the sharing becomes complicated very quickly. Especially as new requirements are being added to the mix.

Now you need to worry about a sharing rule, queue ownership, and manual sharing of records to the guest user.

This is why it is super important that when you design and build solutions you not only consider the requirements today, but also how you will be able to expand functionality in the future, while maintaining the security of your data and usability of the application.

Now there are a couple of issues that you need to consider:

1. **Any partner put into the Global Partner queue will be shared externally with any visitor browsing the public site.**

2. **Any time an account manager shares a strategic partner with the guest user, the partner will be shared externally with any visitor browsing the public site.**

Some questions regarding these issues might be:

1. **What if the internal users assigning partner accounts to the Global Queue do not realize that by sharing with the Global Queue, the partner will now be visible to site-unauthenticated users?**

2. **How will you be able to easily know which partner accounts that are now publicly visible have been manually shared with the guest user?**

3. **How will users know that what is on a strategic account is being shared publicly?**

4. **What if someone forgets a partner was shared, and now they are no longer a strategic account and should no longer be shared?**

You may say, "So what? These are only partners or companies and nothing sensitive is being shared." But let's take this to another level.

What if these partners were not companies but instead consumers leaving reviews?

What if these people could choose to display or not display their personal information publicly?

How can you guarantee someone didn't accidentally share someone's personal information?

How could you easily know who was shared and who was not?

What if the person in the future no longer wanted their information shared?

What kinds of fines could you be facing if you shared someone's personal information without their permission?

As you can see, once you mix the guest user and authenticated Digital Experience user sharing, things start to get quite complicated. You now need to create additional rules to account for both cases, along with exceptions to those rules for edge cases.

If you add the Digital Experience standard Customer license type back into the mix, you also need to worry about setting up the correct **Sharing Sets** so data is shared correctly with standard Customer users, since sharing rules do not apply to the "Customer" license type.

Prior to Salesforce's Winter '20 release, this is how you had to manage sharing data between the guest and authenticated site users. While designing your solution, you need to ensure that you configure your security model in a way that fit both the guest and authenticated users.

As you can imagine, many customers may have inadvertently shared data with the general public without even realizing it. It was just too easy to accidentally expose sensitive data.

At this point I feel that it is important to mention that by no means do I feel Salesforce did anything wrong here by allowing this to happen. The power of Salesforce's platform is the ability to easily configure it at a very granular level. Customers demanded that the platform be flexible to evolve with their business, and with that evolution more and more features were introduced that provided for more flexibility, but along with it more complexity. Shortly, I will discuss what Salesforce did to help reduce the complexity with the guest user sharing.

To reduce some of the complexity, Salesforce has always recommended to configure security using the broadest sharing controls first, then move to the more granular controls. The use of the granular sharing such as manual sharing should only be used as an exception, but not the norm.

Salesforce security features, called **Profiles**, **Permission Sets**, and **Permission Set Groups**, let you control the visibility at the object level, which is one of the broadest ways you can control access to data in Salesforce. If, for example, the public visitors do not have a need to see any data for an object, then you would restrict the guest user from access to that object.

Once that was done, it would not matter if you set the object sharing defaults for the authenticated Digital Experience users to **Public** or even **Public Read/**

Write, since the guest user was restricted from accessing any records in the object. This can also be applied to any other user type in Salesforce as well, since every user in Salesforce must be assigned to a profile.

This was one way that customers could get around the sharing issue for the guest user, but this adds another level of complexity and monitoring for what the guest user can access.

Because of these complexities, or because sometimes customers could not find an easy way to share records to the authenticated users without sharing with the guest user, they would instead create custom components in Salesforce that would use programmatic ways to restrict access to the guest user, so site visitors could only see the specific records.

Customers would remove the default "out-of-the-box" Digital Experience components from the screen layout using the drag-and-drop builder and replace them with their custom components designed to display only the data that guest users could see.

As an additional precaution, they would also remove the ability for someone to execute Salesforce's APIs as the guest user so they could not bypass the user interface screens to get the data.

This approach dates to before Lightning Components were released, when customers would use programmatic ways to control security in Salesforce Visualforce pages. (In case you are unaware, Visualforce pages are a feature of Salesforce that let you build custom webpages in Salesforce.) The key difference was that Visualforce pages run on the server-side whereas Lightning Components run on the client-side. What this means is that in Visualforce all the code that ran was hidden from the user, versus in Lightning much of the code being run is visible to the user in their browser under the covers.

Remember, as noted above, the guest user could still access all the records under the covers. The Lightning user interface only restricted access to what public site visitors could see via the web browser, but not from Salesforce's unpublished Lightning Aura APIs.

This seemed like a solid approach, but there were three major issues that people didn't think or know about:

1. **What if someone accidentally missed something? What if an object was exposed and the out-of-the-box user-interface components were left on the screen, exposing data?**

2. Just because the Salesforce out-of-the-box components were not on the screen, it didn't always mean someone could not get to those pages.

3. Many times, if you knew the correct URL, you could still access these pages, thereby viewing data that was not intended for a user to be able to see.

4. Remember when I mentioned earlier that Salesforce had these "undocumented" APIs used to display data and the layouts for the Lightning Experience?

5. Those APIs could still retrieve the data since the guest user still had access to the records. There was no way to block users from executing those APIs, so anyone that knew how to find and use them could retrieve that data if the user had access.

Because of the various ways you could share data to the guest user, customers had to be very careful to ensure that data was not being exposed to guest users.

The problem was that it was too easy to miss something since Salesforce's security model is so granular and configurable.

Also, creating these custom interfaces didn't solve the problem since these undocumented APIs could still access the data.

This caused many customers to accidentally expose data to the public that was sensitive or even private in nature.

SALESFORCE TO THE RESCUE!

Fast-forward to September of 2019, when Salesforce released a notice that critical changes to Public Sites security were coming in their Winter '20 release.

Salesforce was releasing features that would help better secure the Digital Experience and Public Sites guest user to help avoid accidental data leakage.

Hooray!

Salesforce customers now would have the option to enable these features to lock down data access to the guest user.

The following section highlights the changes made to the Salesforce security model concerning the guest user.

A NEW GUEST SHARING MODEL

Remember earlier we discussed how the power of Salesforce is the flexibility and granularity? Well, Salesforce realized that it was just too easy to accidentally expose data to public visitors through the guest user because there were too many ways to share data and too much access to that data could be granted to unknown or untrusted public visitors.

Customers could share record data to guest users in the following ways:

1. **Using Salesforce sharing rules that could grant full access to records**

2. **Via ownership of Salesforce queues**

3. **Via public groups by adding the guest user to the group**

4. **Manually sharing records to the guest user**

5. **Setting the guest user as the owner of records**

To simplify the guest user sharing model and reduce the risk of data unknowingly being shared to the guest user, Salesforce decided to split the sharing model of the Digital Experience authenticated users and the guest user so that now the guest user would also have its own sharing model for Salesforce objects.

Unlike for other users, once enabled, this new sharing model would default the access level for the guest user to private for every object in Salesforce. This meant that by default, the guest user would not have access to any records.

Additionally, to further simplify the sharing of guest users, customers would no longer be able to add the guest user to queues or public groups, and manually sharing records to the guest user would no longer be supported.

Salesforce also made it so that guest users could no longer own records. Instead, when a record was created by a guest user, that record was automatically assigned to a **Default Owner** for the Digital Experience site.

Record ownership in Salesforce is one of the highest access levels a user can have. Once a user owns a record, they can view, edit, or delete the record.

Furthermore, whenever a user creates a record in Salesforce, they also automatically become the owner. By preventing guest users from owning records, Salesforce also prevented guest users from being granted elevated access to data that would expose that access to public visitors on the site.

This was all great, but what if you still needed to share some data with the guest user, such as in our first example of providing the ability for site visitors to search for a partner or distributor near their location?

If you recall, the guest user now had its own sharing model whereby default access to all object record data was set to **Private**, meaning that the guest user had no access to any record data.

Luckily, Salesforce still allowed us to share record data in **Read Only** mode, so Digital Experience site users could still access data where it made sense.

To do this, Salesforce released a special guest user sharing rule where you can share data to the guest user in **Read Only** mode.

All these changes greatly simplified tracking of how records were being shared with the user since now there was only one way that guest users could be granted access to records: by creating a sharing rule giving **Read-Only** access.

This vastly reduced the chance that sensitive data could be leaked to the public internet and made it much easier for system administrators to know exactly how and which records were being shared with the Digital Experience guest users.

Or so they thought but we will get into that a little later once we get back to our story.

It wasn't enough to lock down the sharing of the record data to the guest user in the Digital Experience sites. There were a couple of other areas that needed some attention as well.

Another highly overlooked but very important area of Digital Experiences regarding data privacy was the sharing of user data within the site.

Prior to the release of the security updates, if you wanted to allow guest users to view all the users within the Digital Experience site, you would enable **the View All Users** permission on the guest user's profile.

The problem with this was that enabling that option also gave the guest user access to all internal users within the Salesforce environment. This, of course, created a major security risk by exposing Salesforce customers' internal users to the public internet.

Also, many people didn't realize when they checked the **View All Users** permission that they were not only sharing the Digital Experience users with the guest user but also with the internal users. Sure, you didn't have to enable that permission. You could also use some of the other sharing mechanisms that existed, such as rule-based sharing or manual sharing, but as was discussed earlier, that got very confusing.

To further simplify the sharing for the guest user and eliminate the risk of internal users being shared with the guest user, Salesforce removed the **View All Users** permission from the guest user's profile and added a new **Guest User Visibility** preference to the Digital Experience site settings that would make all the users within the Digital Experience visible to the guest user.

Another area at risk for exploitation was the custom Salesforce Apex code executed as part of any custom Lightning components developed and placed in the Digital Experience layout.

If you recall, we discussed that many times as a work-around to the sharing, or as a means to bring a site more in line with their company branding, a customer uses Salesforce custom code to develop custom Lightning components that can be used to replace out-of-the-box components.

Many of these components operate in a privileged mode that grants access to more recorded data than the guest user would normally be able to access. This is not always a security risk, as sometimes you need to allow your code to execute elevated actions that a user would not normally be able to perform.

In the next section we will discuss what Salesforce has done to help address this risk.

THE PROBLEM WITH @AURAENABLED

To expose executable code in the Lightning Experience, a developer needs to tag their code methods with the **@AuraEnabled** directive. This alone was not a security risk, but the issue was that once the code had this directive, it could be executable by any user, including the guest user, by employing those unpublished APIs we spoke of earlier from any page on the site.

```
public without sharing class GeneralUtility{

    @AuraEnabled
    public static void
    deleteRecords(List<sobject> records){

        delete records;
    }


    @AuraEnabled
    public static List<Contact>
    getContacts(string searchString){

        return database.query('select id,
        firstName, lastName, email, phone,
        birth_date__c, ssn__c, from Contract
```

```
                where email like %' + searchString +
'%'];
    }
}
```

FIGURE 3. CODE EXAMPLE OF USING @AURAENABLED
TO EXPOSE METHODS IN LIGHTNING AURA
COMPONENTS IN THE LIGHTING EXPERIENCE.

It was basically an all-or-none kind of thing. Either you exposed all your code in a class to every page and user on the site (including the guest user), or you exposed none of it.

Salesforce recognized this was a big security risk, so as part of the guest user security update release, they created a new security feature for code with the @ AuraEnabled directive to be executed within a Digital Experience site by a user: the user's profile had to have the code whitelisted. This ensured that only those users authorized to execute code could do so.

This change was especially important since code can return records or perform database operations such as inserts, updates, and deletes. You definitely would not want to give just anyone the ability to do this.

This was an excellent step in the right direction to help ensure that Salesforce customers' data was not accidentally leaked to public visitors in their Digital Experience sites.

Because these new settings would make data access to guest users much more restrictive, there was a good chance that once these settings were enabled, customers' functionality in their public-facing sites would no longer operate.

To make the transition as smooth as possible, Salesforce even went so far as to present guidance to their customers on what steps they should take in preparation to enable these features since Salesforce was going to start enforcing these new security changes in the Spring '20 release. This meant customers would not have the option not to disable these new security features once Spring '20 was released.

Recommendations by Salesforce included the following:

1. **Create Guest User Sharing Rules for any object where you want to share records with the guest user.**

2. **Add Apex classes to the profiles for any user where those classes must be executed as part of a custom Lightning component for any methods in those classes that use the @AuraEnabled directive.**

3. **Add Without Sharing to any Apex classes where guest users need access to view or**

update records, such as retrieving or updating the shopping cart for anonymous users on an e-commerce site.

4. **To help customers better understand what data was accessible by the guest user, customers were instructed to install a managed package developed by Salesforce to view a Guest User Access Report that displayed all the access granted to guest users and any risks being exposed.**

This package has now been integrated into the core of Salesforce. If you open setup and search for **Guest User Access Report**, you will quickly see what records have been exposed to the guest user for any of your Digital Experience sites.

Additionally, a new managed package has been released that goes even further to detail the security risks for your guest and authenticated users. This package is available for download at https://appexchange. salesforce.com/appxListingDetail?listingId=a0N3A00 000FYkDDUA1.

These recommendations were targeted at helping customers continuing to offer the same functionality in their sites after the enhanced guest user security settings have been enabled.

The problem with these three recommendations was that they also helped to circumvent the very restrictions put in place to protect customer data. In the next section, we will dive further into each of these recommendations and what you can do to reduce your risk and protect your data.

CHAPTER 4

ENSURING CUSTOMER DATA SECURITY

Although these recommendations at the end of the previous chapter themselves are not bad, if used incorrectly, they could potentially expose customer sensitive and private data.

Now let's do a quick recap of what we discussed earlier.

Even if the Salesforce user interface is configured not to show specific elements, there are a number of ways that data can be accessed in a Salesforce Digital Experience. These methods include:

1. **Accessing out-of-the-box Salesforce URLs that display data to the guest user and cannot be hidden.**

2. Executing Salesforce unpublished Lightning APIs that render the Salesforce Lightning interface.

Normally, accessing out-of-the box URLS that cannot be hidden would not be an issue if no data is exposed to the guest user.

Executing unpublished Lightning APIs, however, can create more of a security risk. The Salesforce Lightning experience, which is the user interface for both internal Salesforce users and for Salesforce Digital Experiences, uses various APIs to dynamically render the user interface and display the data. These APIs are not designed to be called directly by a customer, but a potential attacker who knows what they are doing could execute these APIs to retrieve data and execute database operations or even custom code.

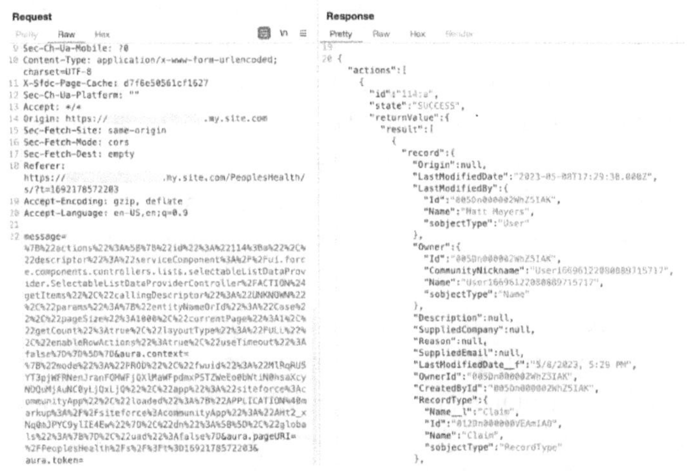

FIGURE 4. EXAMPLE OUTPUT FROM THE LIGHTNING EXPERIENCE UNPUBLISHED APIS.

Therefore, it is especially important to ensure the guest user's access is limited to public-only data and operations since users do not need to log on to execute these operations as the guest user.

Custom Apex code execution could provide an even higher risk since you can access and do pretty much anything with custom code in Salesforce. Great care needs to be taken when developing custom code used in Salesforce Digital Experiences, especially code that could be executed as the guest user, as any person with an internet connection could execute that code.

For years, it has been a common practice by developers to group Apex methods in classes by business function rather than by the user personas that need access to these methods. The issue with this approach is that a class is often exposed via multiple profiles or permission sets when a group of users needs access to only a small number of methods within that class.

The problem with this is that when you give access to a class, you give execution access to every method in the class, not just specific ones. When sharing access to objects or fields, you don't give users access to every object or field; you should take the same approach with methods in classes.

Now imagine a class with a method that needs to be accessed by the guest user, but there are other methods in the same class that only internal users access. Since the guest user needs access to this one method, you grant the guest user access to the class. Without realizing it, you have just granted the guest user access to every method in the class. Now, if those methods are **@AuraEnabled**, this means that any of those methods are now executable by anyone on the public internet.

Take for example, the class below. There are two methods in this class. One is designed to retrieve a specific partner by name to be displayed to public users. The other allows you to delete any record in Salesforce.

Imagine if anyone could execute the method **Delete Records** below, allowing them to delete any record in a Salesforce environment? What if there was a method that also returned customer private information too? What a perfect opportunity for an attacker!

```
public without sharing class GeneralUtility{

    @AuraEnabled
    public static void
    deleteRecords[List<sobject> records]{

        delete records;
    }

    @AuraEnabled
    public static List<Contact>
    getPartners[string partnerName]{

        return database.query['select id, name,
        email, phone from partners__c where
        name like %' + partnerName + '%'];
    }
}
```

FIGURE 5. EXAMPLE OF A BAD PRACTICE INCLUDING MULTIPLE METHODS IN A SINGLE CLASS THAT WOULD BE EXECUTABLE BY USERS OF MULTIPLE ROLES. ALWAYS ORGANIZE METHODS IN A CLASS BY SECURITY FUNCTION AND NOT BY BUSINESS FUNCTION.

To avoid this vulnerability, instead of creating methods in classes by business function, it is better to create methods by security persona, so that users are only granted access to methods that they have a business need to execute.

Notice that I have split out the methods from the class above into two separate classes: one for an admin user persona and another for the guest user. This helps to ensure that the guest user would not have access to execute code that was only meant for an administrative user.

```
public without sharing class
AdminUserGeneralUtility{

    @AuraEnabled
    public static void
    deleteRecord(List<sobject> records){

        delete records;
    }
}
```

FIGURE 6. EXAMPLE OF HOW THIS METHOD FROM FIGURE 5 WAS SPLIT OUT INTO A SEPARATE CLASS ALLOWING ONE THE ABILITY TO ONLY EXPOSE THIS METHOD TO USERS WHO SHOULD HAVE ACCESS TO EXECUTE IT. (IT IS ALSO WORTH NOTING IN THE REAL-WORLD YOU WOULD WANT TO VERIFY THE USER EXECUTING THIS METHOD HAS THE APPROPRIATE ACCESS TO PERFORM THE OPERATION.)

```
public with sharing class
GuestUserGeneralUtility{

    @AuraEnabled
    public static List<Contact>
    getPartners(string partnerName){
```

```
        return database.query['select id, name,
        email, phone from partners__c where
        name like %' + partnerName + '%'];
    }
}
```

FIGURE 7. EXAMPLE OF HOW THIS METHOD FROM FIGURE 5 WAS SPLIT OUT INTO A SEPARATE CLASS ALLOWING ONE TO EXPOSE THIS METHOD TO USERS WHO SHOULD HAVE ACCESS TO EXECUTE IT.

Take this scenario, for example:

You want to allow public unauthenticated users to submit cases through your Salesforce Digital Experience site.

To do this, you need to allow the guest user to create case records and send data from the case records into Salesforce.

Additionally, you want to create a new contact record for the user—if they do not already exist in Salesforce—that could be associated with the case.

Since this is a multistep process that requires searching against all existing contact records in Salesforce, you need to create custom code using an Apex class **without sharing**, providing elevated access to query every existing contact record in Salesforce.

The custom Apex code does the following:

1. **Receives case information such as the subject, description, and customer name and email as input.**

2. **Searches Salesforce for any contact with the supplied email and returns a contact record if it exists.**

3. **Creates a new contact if none was returned.**

4. **Creates a new case in Salesforce and associates it with the contact.**

In this scenario, if an attacker were to execute the Apex method that creates the case, the attacker could potentially flood the customer's Salesforce environment with hundreds, if not thousands, of fake case and contact records.

If they were really sneaky, they could make the cases appear normal but inject malicious URLs and files that users could click on.

Now let's make a slight change. Let's say you want to validate the user's email as soon as they enter their email address into the form and then prepopulate their first name, last name, company, phone, and, just for fun, their birthdate.

Since this would require a different workflow from creating the case, you would create a new Apex code method that takes an email as input and returns a contact record including the contact's first name, last name, email, company, phone, and birthdate.

```
public without sharing class
GuestUserGeneralUtility{

    @AuraEnabled
    public static List<Contact>
    getContact(string email){

        return database.query('select id,
        firstName, lastName, email, account.
        name, birth_date__c from Contact
        where email like %' + email + '%');
    }
}
```

FIGURE 8. EXAMPLE OF A POOR PRACTICE OPENING UP AN AURA PAGE FOR ATTACK. SOMEONE COULD EASILY PERFORM AN AUTOMATED ATTACK USING AN EMAIL DATABASE TO RETRIEVE PRIVATE INFORMATION.

Now, instead of only being able to inject fake cases and contact data into the Salesforce environment, the attacker can pass emails to your new method. If a match is found, they will be able to get the personal and private information of your customers without ever having to authenticate.

Let's expand on this scenario one last time.

Let's say that you want to let your users who do not finish the case submission process finish the submission later without having to log on.

To do this, you create a guest user sharing rule providing read-only access to any case in a **Pending** status and giving the guest user view access to any case that has yet to be completed.

You create a Salesforce automation that emails a link to the submitter of the case. Then they can click on the link to resume the case submission.

Since, as far as you know, the only way to view the case is to use the special link emailed to them, you feel it is not a risk sharing all the **Pending** case records with the guest user.

Also, you have disabled API access on the guest user's profile, so someone cannot use Salesforce APIs to retrieve the data.

Sounds like this is a safe and solid approach, right?

Wrong! You just exposed all your customer's personal information to potential attackers for any case in a **Pending** status.

So, what's wrong with this approach?

- If an attacker knew the correct out-of-the-box Salesforce URLs, they could potentially view a list of all the Salesforce cases visible to the guest user. The attacker could click on each case to get private information.

- Using Salesforce's unpublished Lightning APIs, an attacker could make a call as the guest user to return the entire list of all visible case records. This is even worse than the above scenario because an attacker could automate this attack to retrieve hundreds if not thousands of records.

Now that you understand a potential scenario and how an attacker could gain access to data when Salesforce has not been configured correctly, let's take a deeper look into each of the Salesforce recommendations to share data to the guest user.

GIVE READ-ONLY ACCESS VIA GUEST SHARING RULES

Remember, just because it doesn't seem like you can access this data in the Salesforce user interface doesn't mean the data cannot be accessed. Only use **Guest User Sharing Rules** to give **Read-Only** access to guest users for data that is not sensitive.

For example, you want to provide the list of all your partners and their contact information so potential customers can seek help from these partners.

When sharing data, always ask yourself, "Would I be okay if everyone on the planet was given a full copy of all the data I am sharing?" If this answer is not yes, you should rethink sharing the data because you are giving anyone with an internet connection access to the data.

THE PROBLEM WITH ADDING APEX CLASSES TO THE GUEST USER PROFILE

You now know that an attacker can execute any **@AuraEnabled** method in an Apex class that has been shared with the guest user at will and, even worse, through automation. Ensure that any data returned by the Apex class is not sensitive and passes the same test as above. Are you okay if everyone on the planet sees the data?

I personally suggest that you do not expose any Apex classes to the guest user, as this poses too much of a risk.

If you must expose Apex classes, then make sure that the class methods do not perform any operations that could allow an attacker to introduce malicious data or files into your Salesforce environment. Or, you should have a scrubbing process in place to remove malicious data.

Also, try to build controls into your methods so an attacker cannot keep executing your methods repeatedly, flooding your Salesforce environment with records and malicious data or scripts.

Make sure that Apex methods exposed to the guest user do not perform destructive actions such as deleting or updating records.

Last, organize your Apex classes by security persona and not by business function. Remember, once you share an Apex class to a user profile or permission set, every method in that class is exposed and executable by that user. If those methods use the **@AuraEnabled** flag, then those methods are also exposed to your Digital Experience users.

ADD WITHOUT SHARING TO APEX CLASSES

Adding **Without Sharing** in Apex classes gives a way to operate on data that the guest user or other users would not normally be able to access. This can be very dangerous since it could give a potential attacker elevated access to Salesforce.

Remember the example above, where passing an email to the method would return all the personal information of any contact in Salesforce that matched the email, even if the guest user did not have access to the contact record.

If you must expose Apex classes that use **Without Sharing**, make sure that you first put the appropriate security checks in place to validate the data before performing operations that could put your Salesforce environment at risk.

I once had a customer who created a method that used Without Sharing that took a single parameter of a list of Salesforce IDs, as demonstrated earlier in Figure 6. The method would delete all the IDs without checking if the user making the deletions had the correct access. To make matters worse, this was exposed to the guest user. This meant an attacker could delete virtually every record in the customer's Salesforce environment without ever having to authenticate.

When performing database updates in code, always validate in the code that the user executing the actions have the appropriate access to perform those actions. Many times Salesforce code executes in **System Mode**, which means normal profile security checks are bypassed when the code executes.

Don't make this same mistake!

CHAPTER 5

SOLVING THE PROBLEM

As the meeting ended, I thought to myself, "How could this have happened? It has now been months since Salesforce enforced the guest user security enhancements, locking down the sharing of records with our Digital Experience guest user in our portal."

I took a sip of my now-cold coffee as my stomach rumbled since I still had not eaten anything after the blackened oatmeal incident.

I continued my thoughts. We even followed every recommendation Salesforce provided us, yet this still happened.

I wonder if anyone else besides this ethical hacker figured this out? How much of our customers' private data is now on the dark web? And what will our customers think?

During the call, it was decided that since customers' private information was indeed being exposed, the site would immediately be suspended until the issue could be resolved.

Since this was the company's primary source for customers to submit healthcare applications and claims, a page would be put up informing customers that the site was under maintenance, directing them to call the global call center to submit their application.

The company management expected that this would increase the volume of inbound calls to the center by at least four times, and even with increased staff, customer wait times would, on average, be sixty minutes or greater, and they expected that half of the applicants would get frustrated and go to a competitor instead.

Even worse, healthcare providers submitting claims may not be able to get through in time to make critical decisions for lifesaving operations.

This just went from bad to worse. I wondered how much this would cost the company.

There was now extreme pressure on the team at the highest levels to act quickly to determine what data was being shared and how to bring the site back online without risking the security of our customer's private data.

After meeting with the team, we created a four-step resolution action plan.

STEP 1: IDENTIFY THE HOLE

The first step was to identify the hole in the solution allowing data to be accessed by the Salesforce un-published APIs.

After a thorough analysis of our solution, we found that we had two issues.

1. **Pending applications were being shared with the guest user.**

   So that users who had not yet completed their application or claim could return and finish by using a "secret" link, we created a rule that shared any application with a "Pending" status with the guest user.

   Initially, we did this because Salesforce had recommended that if we needed to share data with the guest user, we should add a sharing rule.

Of course, had we known that the data could have been accessed via an un-documented API, we would have taken a different course of action.

Because of this, we needed to remove this sharing rule so that these pending applications and claims were no longer shared with the guest user but still some-how allowed the customers to access their pending submissions in a more secure way.

2. **Custom Apex without sharing API re-turned sensitive information.**

   We also found that we had custom Apex code that would return an individual's full personal information profile when an email was sent to the code, so we could prefill the application form with the individual's data if it already existed in Salesforce.

   With the undocumented APIs' ability to be executed by just about anyone, this opened up the potential for an attacker to retrieve user personal information by sending a list of emails.

We would need to remove this code as it was also a potential security risk.

STEP 2: PLUG THE HOLE

The second step was to plug the hole in the current intake process so that no submissions with customer information would be shared with the guest user, regardless of whether it had been completed.

We realized that because any data shared with the guest user could still be accessed by these Salesforce Lightning "unpublished" APIs. We could no longer share any record with the guest user, or we would be exposing the data to potential attackers.

We also could not create any custom Apex code that would allow an attacker to retrieve data stored in Salesforce that should not be publicly accessible. The problem was that the business still needed to allow people to submit applications and claims without first creating a log on, or they would see a large drop in completed applications.

In the end, we came up with a compromise that kept our customers' data safe while still accomplishing the business goals.

We created a single-page form that asked the user to complete their basic profile information, including their first name, last name, email, phone, and other basic detail information.

Then, upon submission of the form, we made a new account for the user, if one did not already exist, and created a new submission record associated with the user, not the guest user.

The user was advised to check their email to complete the submission process. They would then click a link that would take them back to Salesforce. At this time, they could set a password for their user account and complete the process.

If, for some reason, the user didn't complete the process, we set up an automated email to remind them to finish later.

This new workflow allowed the user to become invested in the submission process. By sending the automated correspondence, we were able to validate that the email address and the person were real.

Even though this solution required us to create some custom code accessible to the guest user to complete the submission, the record was blocked from anyone on the internal team until the process was completed and the email was validated.

This prevented an attacker from flooding Salesforce with fake submissions that internal users could access. Instead, unless someone completed the process within five business days, the submission was automatically removed from the system.

Unlike what we had before, this new process did not require any sharing rules to share data with the guest user.

In the end, this gave the business the best of both worlds, and they were happy with the outcome, and so was the leadership and security team.

STEP 3: CLEAN UP THE DATA

The third step in the process was to clean up any data that could still be shared with the guest user.

We knew that after we removed the sharing rule, most, if not all records, were no longer being shared with the guest user.

To make sure there were no more open holes, we decided to take it a step further and search for any records in any object in Salesforce where the guest user shared a record or owned a record.

Initially, we didn't expect to find anything since it had been months since Salesforce enabled the features where guest users could not own or be shared any records using manual sharing.

To our surprise, after we ran the searches, we found that we had 3,552 applications in a pending status that the guest user owned and 2,982 contact records that had been manually shared with the guest user.

This was a great catch and a valuable lesson learned about the Salesforce guest user changes that we had yet to realize.

We noticed one thing in common with all these records: they had been created prior to Salesforce enabling the new guest user security features.

When Salesforce enabled the guest user changes, they had not removed any shares where preexisting records were shared with the guest user. They also hadn't changed any records where the guest user was the owner.

STEP 4: VALIDATE AND REACTIVATE

The final step in the process was to validate that everything worked and that we no longer had any data exposed to the public.

Once that was complete, we were able to successfully reactivate the site within one week of the incident.

THIS WAS ONLY THE BEGINNING

You may be thinking to yourself that this doesn't sound all that complicated, and it only took one week to fix.

The fix itself was not that complicated, as in the end it was a single sharing rule that was sharing out records to the guest user, but to implement the fix we had to redesign the application intake process. This required many developers to work day and night until the fix was complete due to the level of impact.

We realized that we may have resolved the immediate issue, but this was only the beginning. We had hundreds of Apex class methods that use the **@AuraEnabled** flag that were shared with both the guest user and authenticated Customer Plus and Partner Digital Experience users. A larger effort was needed to review the code in each of these methods to ensure that someone could not gain unauthorized access to data or perform other destructive actions. This process could take months to review and remediate any issues that are found.

Here are some questions you should be asking yourself:

1. How many Apex classes do you have that are using **@AuraEnabled** where the guest

or other Digital Experience users may have access?

2. How many of them are using **Without Sharing**?

3. Do any of them return potentially sensitive data?

4. Do any of them perform actions such as inserts, updates, or deletes?

5. What could someone do if they were able to execute those methods at will?

6. Who is able to execute these methods?

If you are unable to answer these questions with certainty, I think you too may have a lot of work to do in the future to secure your data.

THE REAL COST OF A DATA BREACH

Unfortunately, this story is all too common among large and small organizations. Did you know that 60 percent of all small businesses that experience a breach will go out of business within six months, and nearly 75 percent of companies have said that they have faced a material disruption in business process due to a data breach?

According to an IBM study, nearly sixty-eight records are exposed every second. Think about that. How many records have been exposed globally while you have been reading this book?

What makes matters worse is that on average, it takes 206 days to detect a breach and another seventy days to recover from that breach. How much would that cost your organization if someone had access to your data without you knowing it for over 206 days? What would your customers think?

When it's all said and done it costs organizations on average $4.36 million globally per breach. In the United States, the cost is over $9 million per breach. This doesn't even consider the cost of repairing a lost reputation. How much would it cost your organization to repair your customers' trust if you allowed their private information to fall into the hands of an attacker who posted it all over the dark web? How many of those customers would go to your competitors? What would that cost?

WHAT CAN BE DONE TO AVOID A BREACH?

All this is pretty scary stuff, but what can you do to stop this from happening to you? Unfortunately, it is impossible to protect yourself completely against a data breach, but there are things you can proactively do to harden your Salesforce environment against attacks.

As the saying goes, "The best defense is a good offense."

1. Use Salesforce Shield Event Monitoring

Event Monitoring is a paid offering by Salesforce that allows you to monitor activity within your Salesforce environment for specific events to help you identify suspicious activity and help stop potential threats.

Some examples of these types of events that can be monitored are:

- **Login Events**

  Know when specific users or types of user login to Salesforce. For example, if you notice a single user is logging into Salesforce hundreds of times within a specific timeframe, this could be a potential attack.

- **Aura Request Events**

  Allows you to know when Apex methods are being executed from Aura or Lightning web components. This is very useful in detecting some of the attacks outlined earlier in the previous chapter.

- **Content Transfer Events**

  Alerts you when someone uploads, downloads, or previews a file in Salesforce. There is no way to stop an authenticated user from uploading files in Salesforce. Luckily the guest user has a switch you can enable to block guest users from uploading files. This event helps you to understand when file data is being accessed or if unauthorized files are being uploaded to your Salesforce environment.

2. Run the Guest & Authenticated User Access Reports

If you recall earlier, I mentioned that Salesforce provides tools that you can run to help you understand what data guest users and authenticated users can access. These reports are very useful in helping you understand what data has been shared to both your guest and authenticated users.

The Guest User Access Report is available by searching setup in Salesforce. The more advanced version requires you to install the managed package located at https://appexchange.salesforce.com/appxListingDetail?listingId=a0N3A00000 FYkDDUA1. Both should be run any time you make changes to your Salesforce security model.

3. Run Salesforce Health Check

Health Check is another built-in Salesforce tool that helps you identify areas of improvement in your Salesforce security configuration. Health Check can also be customized to meet your company's security standards within Salesforce and provides you with a health score for how compliant you are with these standards.

4. Use Salesforce Lightning Web Component Sites

Much of what I have mentioned in this book are targeted at Salesforce "Aura" Lightning Digital Experience sites. Aura sites are built using Salesforce's Lightning Component Aura framework that is a proprietary framework built by Salesforce allowing you to componentize your Salesforce sites.

Instead of continuing to build out the Aura framework, Salesforce has decided to adopt open standards going forward and in Spring of 2019 released a new framework called Lightning Web Components, also known as LWC.

Salesforce built LWC on top of the core open-source Web Component standards and provides only what's necessary to perform well in browsers. Visually this framework looks the same to end-users, but under the covers it functions very differently.

This framework is also secure by design. Unlike the Aura framework where you must include an Apex class **Controller** that exposes any method with the **@AuraEnabled** directive to the entire public site users and Guest User, with LWC you must explicitly expose each method you wish to use for any single component.

Take for example our partners Apex method that we discussed before. Previously in the Aura component, every method in the **GeneralUtility** class would have been exposed to our component, giving access to attackers the **Delete Records** method.

```
public without sharing class GeneralUtility{

    @AuraEnabled
    public static void
    deleteRecords[List<sobject> records]{
        delete records;
```

```
    }

    @AuraEnabled
    public static List<Contact>
    getPartners(string partnerName){

        return database.query('select id, name,
        email, phone from partners__c where
        name like %' + partnerName + '%');
    }
}
```

FIGURE 9. A REMINDER THAT THIS CLASS IS USING POOR PRACTICES THAT COULD EXPOSE A THREAT WHEN USING AURA LIGHTNING COMPONENTS. WHEN USING THIS SAME CLASS WITH LWC, ONLY OUR **GETPARTNERS** METHOD WITHIN OUR **GENERALUTILITY** CLASS HAS BEEN EXPOSED INSTEAD.

```
import { LightningElement, api } from 'lwc';
import getPartnersAPI from '@salesforce/apex/
GeneralUtility.getPartners';

export default class partnersSiteComponent {

    async getPartnerDetails(partnerName){
        return getPartnersAPI(partnerName);
    }
}
```

FIGURE 10. AN EXAMPLE OF HOW LWC EXPOSES ONLY THE METHOD OR METHODS YOU WISH TO USE WITHIN A CLASS AND NOT EVERY METHOD AS WITH AURA LIGHTNING COMPONENTS.

This vastly reduces the risk for potential exposure since you are explicitly and intentionally exposing each Apex method instead of referencing a class that is full of multiple methods that could be exposed.

As part of this framework and to increase the security of Digital Experience sites, Salesforce also released a new type of Digital Experience site that runs on the Web Component framework instead of the Aura framework. Most importantly, the attack that I've outlined in this book using the unpublished APIs is much more difficult to achieve with LWC sites than with Aura sites. A large part of that is because of the intentional nature and locked down by default approach to the framework as described above.

I highly suggest that you consider migrating any of your existing Aura Lightning Experience sites to web component sites to further secure your data. I'm not saying that someone couldn't take advantage of these new type of sites and components, but it would be much more difficult.

While these tools can help you to proactively protect your Salesforce environment, securing your Salesforce environment to prevent data breaches really needs to start at the program level. You need to ensure that you have the correct governance controls in place and that there are checks and balances and reviews before any changes are deployed to your production environments.

CHAPTER 7

CONCLUSION

The week after the ethical hacker told us how inse-cure our Salesforce data was had to have been one of the most stressful of my career, and I hope that you will never have to live through anything like that.

In the end, we discovered that only a couple legiti-mate attacks had taken place, and only a relatively small amount of customers' private information had potentially been leaked.

Although this didn't make the situation better, it could have been much worse. Luckily, nobody was fired or sued, but this did result in an entirely new level of oversight for our releases and business.

We now follow Salesforce Well-Architected principles, ensuring we build trusted, easy, and adaptable solu-tions. Each release is carefully architected, planned, and reviewed by a highly experienced Salesforce ar-chitect who understands Salesforce security, ensuring

Salesforce security best practices are followed to help avoid any future data leaks or breaches.

I highly recommend that you implement something similar in your Salesforce program if you have not already done so. This could save your company and your job.

In case you have not yet heard of Salesforce Well-Architected, I have included an overview of it as a bonus at the end of this book.

Even with something like Salesforce Well-Architected in place, there is still a possibility that problems may be overlooked, and maybe that is because you didn't know that particular gap was an issue. Because of this, it is a good idea to research constantly to understand the latest threats and features available to secure your organization.

 Luckily there is a resource you can use to stay up to date on the latest Salesforce security best practices so you know what you need to be aware of to protect your data. Working with my team, we release weekly blogs related to Salesforce security threats and best practices, which can be found by going to https://www.ezprotect.io/resources.

For me, this was a monumental learning experience to understand the history of the guest user security in

Salesforce Digital Experiences and the current security best practices that all Salesforce customers should follow in Salesforce Digital Experiences and Salesforce as a whole.

As I continued this journey, I discovered that this is merely the tip of the iceberg. Attackers are becoming more and more insidious, and technology and business requirements are ever evolving. You need to evolve with them to ensure that you are always one step ahead instead several steps behind.

I hope this book has helped you better understand how to protect yourself from data leaks and attacks in your Salesforce Digital Experiences and aids in your improved overall security posture in Salesforce.

APPENDIX A: SALESFORCE WELL-ARCHITECTED

Just like you expect architects to have a framework and methodology to design homes, office buildings, and bridges, you would want your Salesforce program to have a framework that helps you to build secure, scalable implementations, driving value for your customers.

You would want to trust that the bridge you drive on to get to work every day is stable, secure, and built according to a well-thought-through design specification. You would not want to worry about how many cars the bridge could hold, or whether someday the bridge would become obsolete, requiring you to find a new way to work.

You would want the same to be true about your Salesforce implementation.

It is because of these customer expectations that Salesforce has designed the Well-Architected framework.

The Salesforce Well-Architected framework is centered on building healthy solutions, or improving the health of existing solutions, helping architects and organizations to prioritize better where they should be spending their time road mapping and designing solutions on the Customer 360 platform.

The framework provides prescriptive guidance and much-needed examples of anti-patterns and patterns that can be followed while designing solutions. These patterns are based on the knowledge of implementation experts and product teams working together throughout the Salesforce ecosystem.

As a customizable platform, it is essential for architects to emphasize the right direction. The Well-Architected framework is centered on three pillars of what Salesforce solutions should be to help point architects and customers in the right direction.

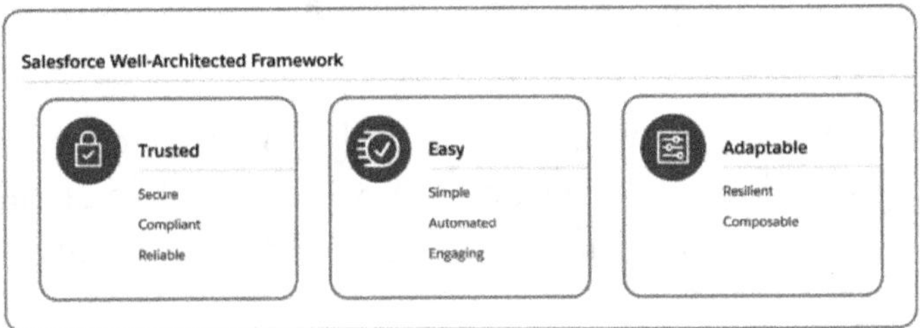

FIGURE 11. SALESFORCE WELL-ARCHITECTED FRAMEWORK CORE PILLARS. FEBRUARY 16TH, 2024. DIAGRAM. SALESFORCE ARCHITECTS. HTTPS://ARCHITECT.SALESFORCE.COM/.

1. **Trusted**: Trust is one of the core values of Salesforce. Customers should be able to trust that the data stored within Salesforce is secure and that the solution complies with regulations and security guidelines for every implementation.

2. **Easy**: Solutions should be able to quickly deliver value. They should be intentional and easy to maintain. They should be automated with clear logic and aligned to drive business value while adhering to data integrity. They should be engaging, streamlined, and helpful to end users.

3. **Adaptable**: As every business keeps evolving with changing needs and trends, implemented Salesforce solutions must be able

to keep up. The solution should be able to evolve as the business evolves.

The Salesforce Well-Architected framework emphasizes helping professionals "how to think like an architect" to build safe, scalable, and healthy solutions.

The fundamental flexibility of Salesforce has been one of the challenges customers face while creating Salesforce solutions. You might be able to extend a prebuilt solution for one, but for another poorly designed solution, you might need to wipe the slate clean and build a completely new, customized application.

What specific technology choices you'll make will entirely depend upon your unique business needs. So, while working with all those distinct features and technologies, it can be tough to evaluate what will contribute to building the long-term health of the Salesforce solution.

To overcome this challenge, Well-Architected provides guidance and insights from experienced Salesforce architects, product managers, and evangelists, so you can use their recommendations and opinions to validate your ideas. The framework allows you to get the right guidance from experts, thus helping you build trusted, easy, and adaptable solutions.

The introduction of the Salesforce Well-Architected framework has brought about a profound transformation in how customers create Salesforce solutions, equipping them with the essential guidance and support necessary to architect secure and scalable solutions.

By strongly emphasizing the pillars of trusted, easy, and adaptable solutions, this framework empowers customers to prioritize critical aspects, such as data security, expedited value delivery, and adaptability to evolving business requirements.

With the framework, Salesforce customers can effectively build healthy solutions that inspire trust, are user-friendly, and evolve alongside the changing demands of businesses.

To learn more about the Salesforce Well-Architected framework, visit https://architect.salesforce.com.

APPENDIX B: HOW DOES WELL-ARCHITECTED HELP TO PREVENT DATA BREACHES?

The first principle of Salesforce Well-Architected focuses on building trusted solutions. By trust, they mean creating secure, compliant, and reliable solutions.

BEFORE ANYTHING, A SALESFORCE SOLUTION SHOULD BE SECURE

For a Salesforce solution to be secure, it must protect stakeholders and an organization's data. When you think about a secure architecture, you want the user accessing a system to be who they say they are, to allow them to access only the necessary data, and to protect that data from exposure.

Salesforce focuses on fostering the trust of its customers and securing the platform. This is what maintains that commitment. It is always a cornerstone for Salesforce to preserve the privacy and security of data. Architects who design and build solutions on the Customer 360 platform should do the same.

Just because Salesforce provides the tools to build a secure solution doesn't mean the solution is secure.

"With great power comes great responsibility."

It is up to you to ensure that solutions that you build on the Salesforce platform are secure. The power is in your hands. Your users and customers are counting on you.

The framework specifically focuses on helping you make your Salesforce organization secure. One of the most important goals for an organization is to assess Salesforce's built-in security features and depending on the unique business requirements and risk, use those features to build a secure and compliant architecture.

For secure solutions, Salesforce Well-Architected focuses on three parameters:
Organizational security
Session security
Data security

ORGANIZATIONAL SECURITY

Organizational security centers on protecting the system from unauthorized access. Strong organizational security means only authorized and validated users can access the system.

You must focus on authentication and authorization to maintain organizational security and know the difference between them to control access to Salesforce properly.

Some key recommendations provided by Salesforce through the framework to maintain authorization and authentication include the following:

- **Use Multifactor Authentication (MFA)**: Salesforce requires MFA for all user interfaces, or UI-based log-ons. Along with the password, at least one additional identification factor should always be required, such as a one-time password through an authenticator or a hardware-based security device.

- **Create Strong Password Policies**: Salesforce recommends creating strong password policies to require users to create safer passwords for log-ons, so they can't be easily compromised.

- **Enable Single Sign-On (SSO)**: Enabling SSO allows users to employ only one set of credentials to access multiple applications. This creates a single kill point to disable user access to these applications. This is especially important when a user's account has been compromised, such as with a credential-stuffing attack. Be careful when implementing SSO as this also could provide an attacker with an easy access point to all of your applications. SSO combined with MFA is always a recommended best practice to protect your data and systems.

- **Using Permission Sets/Groups**: Permission sets and permission set groups help to control and better manage user data access and what they can do. Salesforce recommends moving permissions away from profiles to permission sets and permission set groups, as this allows administrators to more easily understand what permissions are being granted to users and allows for separation of permissions by application or role.

There are many other recommendations, such as API access control, OAuth scopes, and using organization-wide defaults (OWDs). To learn more about some of the other recommendations, visit the Salesforce Well-Architected Trusted overview by going to https://architect.salesforce.com/well-architected/trusted/overview.

SESSION SECURITY

Session security is based on understanding what a session is and how to secure it so that user sessions are not hijacked, giving unrestricted access to attackers.

Sessions are initiated when a user gains access to Salesforce after successful authentication, enabling the platform to create specific requests and responses for a particular user.

Like most modern web applications, Salesforce uses sessions and tokens to track each user's identity and other information across requests.

To secure sessions and tokens, Salesforce suggests different methods such as these:

- Knowing how Salesforce classifies different session types and how they map to different user personas

- Controlling the way sessions are originated (such as with built-in session protection to avoid attacks like clickjacking, content sniffing, forgery, spoofing, and more)

- Controlling activities for sensitive operations that require higher session-level security

- Using time-outs to manage inactive user sessions and preventing or limiting the ability for dormant sessions to be hijacked

DATA SECURITY

Regarding data security, the framework focuses on protecting data from corruption, unauthorized access, or any accidental deletion. Data security emphasizes protecting data, whether at rest or in transit.

When you maintain strong data security, it helps to reduce risks related to unauthorized access to your Salesforce solution. When improving data security, you must understand how data is accessed and what is considered data in Salesforce.

Salesforce Well-Architected emphasizes maintaining strong data security, starting with the following:

- **Maintaining Sharing and Visibility**: A key to maintaining data security involves the control of users' data access within Salesforce. You can use a security matrix that maps your business operations with different user personas. Applying the principle of least privilege, configuring user access rules to data helps to prevent accidental data leakage. You can also set the OWDs to **Private** for maximum security and control.

- **Encryption**: Another way to ensure data security is to enable encryption to convert your readable data into an encoded format to make it indecipherable. Only authenticated users with a key would be able to decipher it. Salesforce uses Transport Layer Security (TLS), which helps to secure all sessions and requires that clients use HTTPS to meet the specific standards for security.

- It's the best practice to encrypt your data that is at rest. Salesforce offers two options for at-rest data encryption depending on the level of security required by your organization:

1. **Hyperforce Salesforce-Managed Encryption**: With the introduction of Hyperforce, Salesforce automatically encrypts customer data using Salesforce-managed keys.

2. **Salesforce Shield**: For those customers who require more advanced and customizable encryption, Salesforce offers a product called Salesforce Shield that allows for customer-managed keys that customers can create or destroy and enables further encryption beyond what is available on Hyperforce.

SALESFORCE SOLUTIONS SHOULD BE COMPLIANT

The Salesforce Well-Architected framework states that for a Salesforce solution to be compliant, it should follow all the legal and ethical guidance while keeping the solution auditable and measurable.

Legal Adherence

To ensure that the Salesforce solution follows legal adherence, it should maintain data privacy and localization.

- **Data Privacy**: Centered on controlling who can access their personally identifiable information (PII). You might have to change your sharing and visibility model to adhere to data privacy rules. Salesforce offers data privacy features to help tag data that contains PII.

- **Localization**: Related to adapting to a particular culture, look, or language for your Salesforce solution while following region-specific regulations. You must ensure that the relevant data to a specific region stays in its separate organization while avoiding data replication.

ETHICAL STANDARDS

These standards focus on following the guidelines for companies and individuals to use the Salesforce data based on a moral standpoint centered on people, process, and technology. People prefer to do business with organizations they trust, and people trust organizations that act ethically and morally and follow the policies that they set forth.

To help promote ethical standards across a company, you should do the following:

1. **Be aware of unintended consequences:** Test both the happy and negative paths. Don't always assume everything will work the way you expect.

2. **Embed ethics into your company's acceptable use policy and culture:** It is your duty to work with the legal team and business stakeholders to ensure your solution

aligns with the company's values, showing your commitment to building trust with your customers.

3. **Use inclusive language:** Doing this ensures that everyone feels like part of the solution and no one feels left out. People feel and understand things in different ways. Design your solution with understanding and sensitivity, taking into consideration the habits and practices that could lead to exclusion.

LIKE DRIVING ON THE BRIDGE, SALESFORCE SOLUTIONS SHOULD BE RELIABLE

To make the Salesforce solution reliable, it is essential to focus on the fact that it should work dependably and effectively. The "Well-Architected" framework centers on three aspects when it comes to making the solution reliable:

- **Availability**: Availability relates to the percentage of time for which the solution remains operational. This involves conducting a thorough risk assessment for your Salesforce solutions to assess the impact severity. After that, you'll prioritize your risks and follow the failure-mitigation plan to fix the issue before any harm is done.

- **Performance**: Performance is centered on assessing the overall processing capacity of the Salesforce solution. To maintain the performance, the framework specifies that the architect focuses on two aspects: throughput optimization and latency optimization.

- **Scalability:** Scalability involves the ability of the solution to keep improving and performing as the company keeps evolving. To make the Salesforce solution scalable, the Salesforce architect should focus on three aspects: data model optimization, data volume management, and testing at scale.

USING THE WELL-ARCHITECTED FRAMEWORK IN THE REAL WORLD

At this point, you may be thinking it's all very well to know in theory, but how can the Well-Architected framework help you and how do you put this information into practice in the real world?

Think of the Well-Architected framework as a guide providing you with lots of resources and best practices that you could and maybe should follow. But truly, it is up to you how you use it to apply to your business.

The framework goes beyond only technical controls and focuses on business process controls and policies that should be implemented to enforce them. The framework should be built into your daily life and should be an integral part of your Salesforce program and release management process.

The Well-Architected framework is not a one-size-fits-all. There are many best practices and guides that may or may not apply to your business. Every business has a different level of risk. Some controls may not be appropriate for your level of risk. Some may be overkill, whereas others may not go far enough.

Before you start implementing the framework, you should perform a mapping exercise of the personas who will be accessing Salesforce, what key requirements they need, and what level of risk they pose to your organization. Think about both internal and external personas. For example, one persona could be a potential attacker, whereas another could be a business user. Both could pose a potential risk to the organization.

Additionally, just because you should implement a control or best practice doesn't mean you can. There may be many restrictions you need to navigate, such as budget or the capacity of your end users.

For example, one of the students I coached told me how she wanted to implement MFA for their Digital Experience site, where users would log on to create financially binding orders. The problem was that many of their users were elderly and didn't own a smartphone device. In this case, even though the framework prescribes that MFA should be implemented, you cannot.

Does that mean you should leave the site vulnerable? Of course not!

It would be best if you started to think about how else you could employ an MFA solution without using an authenticator or one-time password application. Maybe you could instead prompt the users for different pieces of information that only they would know.

I hope you see that the framework is just that, a framework, prescribing the best practices that should be used, but you may need to think outside the box about how that framework applies to your business and in what cases.

A WELL-ARCHITECTED SECURE SOLUTION

I hope you realize how valuable the Salesforce Well-Architected framework could be to your organization to help drive the creation of secure Salesforce solutions, and how you can prevent similar breaches of your company's or clients' websites.

Specifically, if we had been following the Salesforce Well-Architected framework in designing our solutions, maybe we could have avoided the data breach described in the prologue.

Well-Architected is not the end-all solution, as it merely provides you with the guidance and resources needed to build secure Salesforce solutions. It is up to your organization to interpret and implement these recommendations in your security program based on your organization's level of risk.

BONUS #1: RECOMMENDED BEST PRACTICES FOR SECURING YOUR SALESFORCE DATA IN DIGITAL EXPERIENCES AND SITES

SALESFORCE SHARING SETTINGS

1. **Set Default External Access to Private for All Objects**

   It is the best practice to always set security defaults in Salesforce to the most restrictive and then open access as needed.

It is highly recommended to set the **Default External Access** to **Private** for all objects. This sets the default so that no Digital Experience or site users have access to any records that they do not own or were not shared with them.

You can then grant access to users for records that they need to view or edit using sharing rules or other record-sharing features.

2. Routinely Review All Sharing Rules for Guest Users

Salesforce allows administrators to create custom sharing rules to share records with, at most, read-only access to guest users.

You should routinely review your sharing rules to ensure that they are only sharing records that are publicly accessible with the guest user.

Remember: Just because the records are displayed via the Salesforce user interface does not mean that an attacker cannot view the records via other means. If a guest user has access to records in Salesforce, anyone can see those records on the public internet.

Remember the test. Ask yourself if you are okay with everyone in the world seeing those records—because they can.

Salesforce now offers a built-in tool called the **Guest User Sharing Rule Access Report** that can be found under **Setup** in Salesforce. This tool is very helpful in auditing what records are visible to the guest user in each of your Digital Experience sites.

3. Disable Portal and Site User Visibility

Users in customer or partner portals and sites can see each other by default, regardless of the organization-wide defaults. This can expose user data.

By enabling these features, users cannot see each other, thereby hiding user data that should not be exposed.

You should only enable these options if you have a portal or site where all users need to see each other. If only a subset of users needs to see each other, consider using sharing rules instead of enabling this option.

4. Enable Require Permission to View Record Name in Lookup Fields

Lookup fields in Salesforce typically display the record name of the related record in the lookup field. By default, if a user does not have access to the related record, they would still be able to see the name of the record in the lookup field.

In some cases, this may be okay, but consider cases such as system fields that show the names of users or other lookups that may expose sensitive data if the name of a record contains it.

This is why it's a best practice to enable the **Require permission to view record names in lookup fields** to necessitate that a user has view access to the related record of a lookup to view the name of the record in the lookup field.

5. Disable Standard Report Visibility

By default, users can view reports created using Salesforce out-of-the-box report types. This could cause data to be exposed to users where they normally would not have access.

To avoid accidental exposure of data to internal and external users, it's best to disable the setting **Standard Report Visibility**.

6. Secure Guest User Record Access

This setting enables a separate sharing model for the guest user from the site and Digital Experience authenticated users. This data model allows default sets of all object visibility to be set to private.

Sharing rules can be used to provide, at most, read-only visibility to records for the guest user, but use extreme caution when doing this.

Salesforce now enforces that this option be enabled and does not allow customers to disable it. If you see this option is disabled for whatever reason, immediately contact Salesforce to enable it.

7. Remove Guest Ownership for Any Preexisting Records

As of the Spring '20 Salesforce release, guest users cannot own new records or be assigned ownership of an existing record. This ensures that records cannot be accidentally shared with guest users. This change was part of the Summer '20 security enhancements for the guest user.

While the guest user cannot own new records, if the guest user owned any record
prior to the Spring '20 release, then they
would still be the owner of these records.

I highly recommended that if your site guest
user owned any records prior to the Spring '20
release, you change the owner of to another
internal user. This will prevent any leakage of
data created prior to the Spring '20 release.

Even if you intend to share these records
with the guest user, it is a better practice
to change the owner of those records to
an internal user and create a guest user
sharing rule instead of sharing those records directly with the guest user.

SALESFORCE FILE SETTINGS

8. Disable Allow Site Guest Users to Upload Files

By default, guest users in sites and Digital
Experiences are not allowed to upload files.

Files can contain viruses, malware, ransomware,
or malicious scripts. Salesforce does not scan
files for viruses, so it is a best practice only to allow users you know to upload files to Salesforce.

Since guest users are not authenticated, allowing them to upload files introduces a high risk. With this option enabled, an attacker could easily navigate to your site, upload a virus, and then gain control of your systems and customer data.

Never enable this option unless you have other controls in place, such as a virus-scanning service that will review your uploaded Salesforce files for viruses.

Adaptus offers a virus-scanning solution for Salesforce called EzProtect that will ensure that all your files are safe before your users download them. To learn more, please visit https://www.ezprotect.io.

SALESFORCE DIGITAL EXPERIENCES SETTINGS

The following security settings are recommended in each of your Salesforce Digital Experiences.

Preferences

1. Enable Show Nicknames

With this setting disabled, Salesforce Digital Experiences will display the user's first and last names on your site wherever a user field is displayed.

To hide the first and last name of users on the site, you must enable this feature, which will replace the user's first and last name with their nickname instead, protecting their real names.

2. Disable Give Guest Users Access to Public Chatter API Requests

You should only allow authenticated users to participate in Chatter and discussion threads.

Allowing Chatter discussion threads to be displayed to guest users can be accomplished by creating custom Visualforce and Salesforce Lightning components. In order for this to work you need to give the guest user access to make Chatter API requests.

Since this API allows guest users the ability to view Chatter discussion threads, this could open a door for attackers to potentially gain access to view discussion thread data that you normally wouldn't want exposed.

Prior to enabling this feature, make sure that you fully understand the implications and risks. Remember, just because it is not displayed in the user interface doesn't mean that an attacker couldn't gain access to it in a different way.

It best to disable this setting to prevent an attacker from accessing Chatter discussion thread information.

3. Be Careful When Enabling the Direct Messages Setting

Direct messaging in Salesforce Digital Experiences allows users to send direct messages to each other.

Although these direct messages are private to the users, on the back end of Salesforce, these messages show up as private Chatter feeds. Normally, only these users would be able to see their private feeds, but if a developer is using Apex to develop a custom Visualforce Page or Lightning component, since the code runs in system mode, the code could gain access to these private messages.

If the developer is not careful, they could accidentally expose this data to other users.

Unless you have a rigorous process to ensure that developers are not accidentally exposing data in their code, it is best that you disable this feature, so you do not risk exposure of private messages between users.

4. Allow the Guest User to See Other Members of This Site

This setting was released by Salesforce to lock down what guest users can access.

With this setting disabled, guest users cannot view user data for other users within your Digital Experience that your guest user is a member of.

This protects your Digital Experience user information from anyone on the public internet viewing their data.

It is a best practice always to enable this feature to protect your user's personal information and privacy.

5. Set the Default Record Owner for Guest Users

In Salesforce, any user who owns a record has full access to view, edit, or, in most cases, even delete a record.

By default, whenever a user creates a record, that user becomes the owner and gains full access.

To protect your data and your customer's data, Salesforce made it so that guest users cannot own records, even if they created the record.

Instead, an internal user is set to be the default owner of any record in Salesforce.

Make sure that you set the default owner to a user who can view, edit, or delete any record the guest user creates.

Many customers set this user as a special user dedicated to the Salesforce Digital Experience. This is a best practice, provided you have additional licenses.

Otherwise, set this to a user who is a system administrator and has **View All Data** and **Modify All Data** permissions since they would be able to see these records regardless of ownership status.

6. **Allow Only Certain File Types to Be Uploaded in a Digital Experience**

The **Allow only these file types** setting permits you to restrict the extensions for the files allowed to be uploaded to a Digital Experience.

Since certain types of files, like executables, are at higher risk of containing viruses and other threats, you should always restrict users to only upload file types that are lower risk, such as images and PDFs.

When using this setting, please be aware that this would not stop someone from being malicious, as this only blocks file uploading by extension or MIME-type. Attackers can change the extension or spoof the MIME-type of a file to upload a high-risk file. This setting will, however, block normal users from uploading most high-risk files.

If you wish to block even malicious users from uploading high-risk files, consider using a virus-scanning application for Salesforce that can white-list or blacklist files based on their true type and not just their extension.

Adaptus offers a virus-scanning solution for Salesforce called EzProtect that will ensure all your files are safe before your users download. It allows you to white-list or blacklist to guarantee high-risk files are not accessible to your users. To learn more, please visit https://www.ezprotect.io.

7. Routinely Review the Profile Permissions for the Guest User and External Users

Just as your internal users have a profile to control what objects they can see and do in Salesforce, Guest Users and your Digital Experience and site external users also have a profile that controls what they can see and do.

You should review the permissions for these users on a routine basis to ensure that your guests and external users do not have more access than what is needed and they are not being granted access to something that would compromise the integrity of your Salesforce and customer data.

Specifically, you should pay attention to the following settings on the profiles:

1. **Object Settings:** These settings specify what level of access (create, update, and delete) users are granted at the object level in Salesforce and what fields for that object are visible on the layouts and through the Salesforce APIs.

2. It is a best security practice by default to set all objects in the **Object Settings Object Permissions** to **No Access** for guest users

unless there is a reason that the guest user would need access to that object.

3. **App Permissions:** These settings provide elevated access to Salesforce out-of-the-box applications. Typically, these are not administrative functions.

4. **Apex Class Access**: It is important to be careful of this setting, especially regarding guest users. Developers can create methods in Apex classes that use the **@AuraEnabled** directive. This directive means that the Apex method is exposed and usable from the Lightning Experience, including those unpublished APIs discussed earlier.

   Salesforce blocks those methods from being executed if the class is not added to the Apex Class Access list on the user's profile.

   It is essential that you make sure you only add classes that users need to execute within this list.

   Also, make sure you only include methods in each class with this directive that should be exposed together because it is all or none.

Attackers familiar with the Salesforce Lightning undocumented APIs can easily execute any of your Apex classes exposed in this way, so always double-check for your guest users that you are okay with anyone from the public internet executing any method exposed on the guest user profile in the Apex class list.

It would be best if you also carefully reviewed the code on any methods exposed to the guest user to make sure they could not be subject to injection or other types of exploitation and that these methods do not return any sensitive data.

As a better practice, migrate all of your Lightning Aura Components to Lightning Web Components, since LWC provide a much higher level of security when it comes to accessing Apex code.

Migrate your Lightning Aura Digital Experience sites to Lightning Web Component sites for increased security.

5. **Visualforce Page Access:** Similar to Apex Class Access, the Visualforce Page Access section allows a Digital Experience user to execute and view Visualforce pages on the

site. Make sure that only pages the user should access are added to this section.

6. **Flow Access:** Like Apex Class Access, Flow Access grants users the ability to execute Salesforce Flows.

   Be very careful of the types of Flows and operations that you expose to your guest and external users in your Digital Experiences because, just like Apex classes, Flows elevate or even can run with system admin privileges. You wouldn't want a public user invoking this directly without having the proper safeguards in place.

7. **System Permissions:** System permissions apply across Salesforce applications and in many cases, allow users to perform administrative-level functions.

   Pay special attention to any system permissions enabled for Digital Experience external users, especially the guest user.

   Best practice is to uncheck all system permissions for the guest user except for the **Password Never Expires** since guest users don't technically have a password.

8. **Session Settings:** For your authenticated users, you should always employ the **Session Times Out After** setting, so users are required to log on if they are not active after a period of time.

   You should consult with your company's internal policy, but it is typically recommended to time out a user's session after fifteen or thirty minutes of inactivity and set a maximum session lifetime of twenty-four hours or less.

9. **Password Policies:** Just as you set password policies for your internal users, you should also set default password policies for your site and Digital Experience authenticated users. The recommended password policy settings are as follows:

   a. User passwords expire in ninety days.

   b. Enforce password history of at least the last ten.

   c. Set a minimum password length of at least twelve characters.

d. Set the password complexity to include numbers, uppercase letters, lowercase letters, and special characters.

e. Set the maximum invalid log-on attempt to three at the most.

f. Set the effective lockout period after the maximum log-on attempts have been reached to thirty minutes.

BONUS #2: HOW TO ETHICALLY HACK YOUR SALESFORCE DIGITAL SITE TO PROTECT YOUR DATA

Are you curious how the ethical hacker was able to use the Salesforce Lightning unpublished APIs to access my customer's private data?

Are you concerned that your Salesforce Digital Experience might not be as secure as you think?

Well, you are in luck! I specially prepared a YouTube video that walks you through step-by-step how the ethical hacker was able to penetrate my customer's Salesforce Digital Experience site.

In fact, in this video, I actually hack my public help customer portal in my own Salesforce production environment.

HTTPS://GO.EZPROTECT.IO/HACK-SALESFORCE-SITES

BONUS #3: WHAT'S THE BIG DEAL ABOUT VIRUSES IN SALESFORCE AND WHY SHOULD YOU CARE?

There are several ways that attackers could potentially steal your data and penetrate your Salesforce environment.

As you have learned in this book, misconfiguring your Salesforce environment is one of those paths, but there is another way that is often overlooked.

Files uploaded to your Salesforce environment are not being scanned for viruses and other threats. For customers using Digital Experiences, this is an especially high risk since people you do not know or control have the ability to upload and share files with your users and customers.

Most people who are not security professionals are unaware of exactly what a virus can do and why they should care. In this bonus video, I explain precisely why you should care and what you can do about it. Enjoy!

HTTPS://GO.EZPROTECT.IO/
WHAT-IS-THE-BIG-DEAL-ABOUT-VIRUSES-IN-SALESFORCE

REFERENCES

Bachrach, Nitty. "Abusing Misconfigured Salesforce Communities for Recon and Data Theft." *Data Security* (blog). Varonis. April 30, 2023. https://www.varonis.com/blog/abusing-salesforce-communities#:~:text=This%20guide%20explains%20how%20an%20attacker%20can%20exploit,default%20owner%20for%20records%20created%20by%20guest%20users.

Doroftei, Andreea. "Well-Architected: Dreamforce Highlights for Salesforce Architects." Salesforce Ben. September 26, 2022. https://www.salesforceben/dreamforce-highlights-for-salesforce-architects.

IBM. "Cost of a Data Breach 2022 Report." 2022. https://www.ibm.com/account/reg/us-en/signup?formid=urx-51643.

Salesforce Well-Architected. Secure Overview. Last modified December 2022.

https://architect.salesforce.com/well-architected/
trusted/secure.

Salesforce Well-Architected. Trusted Overview. Last
modified July 2022.
https://architect.salesforce.com/well-architected/
trusted/overview.

RESOURCES

Here are some articles and other resources that I think you may find helpful.

Salesforce Communities Could Expose Business Sensitive Information
https://www.infosecurity-magazine.com/news/sales-force-expose-business

Salesforce Guest User Log Analysis
https://appomni.com/resources/aolabs/salesforce-guest-user-log-analysis

Authenticated and Guest User Access Report and Monitoring
https://appexchange.salesforce.com/appxListingDetail?listingId=a0N3A00000FYkDDUA1

Salesforce Lightning: An in-depth look at exploitation vectors for the everyday community
https://www.enumerated.ie/index/salesforce

Salesforce Lightning Design System
https://www.lightningdesignsystem.com

Salesforce Spring '20 Community Guest User Apocalypse
https://katiekodes.com/salesforce-spring-20-guest-user

Salesforce Well-Architected
https://architect.salesforce.com

ABOUT THE AUTHOR

Matt **Meyers** is a Salesforce Certified Technical Architect (CTA), Salesforce security and Well-Architected advocate, and frequent presenter at Salesforce Dreamin' conferences such as CactusForce, Buckeye Dreamin', Architect Dreamin', Life Sciences Dreamin', and others. Matt has dedicated the past eighteen years of his career to learning, implementing, and teaching others about Salesforce.

With over twenty-three years of experience in the tech world, Matt has always been fascinated by technology and business. This cultivated his desire and passion for learning about Salesforce, as he was convinced this was the perfect culmination of both.

"I started out as a Salesforce developer and quickly tried to grasp onto anything I could to learn as much as I could about it. I realized early on that this was the key to growing my career to where I wanted to go and live the lifestyle I always wanted."

With a clear mindset of what he wanted to achieve, Matt quickly gained his first certifications, which helped him to realize that he could not grow any further in his current position, prompting the decision to join HCL, a global consulting company, where he began his career as a Salesforce consultant.

Matt's passion for Salesforce technology saw him study and earn numerous Salesforce certifications. This helped expand his industry network significantly, and he connected with a recruiter who saw him secure an opportunity at Salesforce.

"I then started out as a customer-facing architect in Salesforce services, helping some of Salesforce's largest customers implement Salesforce. I was constantly learning and being challenged, and I eventually acquired the highest certification: Certified Technical Architect," Matt explains.

Matt's hard work and unparalleled work ethic allowed him to grow and scale into a director role, managing all of Salesforce's program architects in the public sector. At that time, he decided to go independent and establish his own company.

Over the years, Matt has had many struggles and setbacks but eventually grew to become a true expert in his field. He now shares his story, seeking to connect with and help others on the same journey that he started, hoping that they can stay with him no matter where they go as they progress through their careers. He aims to help them through their journeys and see them through to success so they, too, can succeed in their Salesforce careers and exceed in their life goals.

www.ingramcontent.com/pod-product-compliance
Lightning Source LLC
Chambersburg PA
CBHW061539120726
48001CB00004B/1635